Amazing
Animal
Disguises

EYEWITNESS JUNIORS

Amazing Animal Disguises

WRITTEN BY
SANDIE SOWLER

ALFRED A. KNOPF · NEW YORK

Conceived and produced by
Dorling Kindersley Limited

Editor Bernadette Crowley
Art editor Mark Regardsoe
Senior art editor Julia Harris
Senior editor Helen Parker
Production Shelagh Gibson

Illustrations by Ruth Lindsay and Jane Gedye
Photography by Jerry Young, Carl Shone, Jane Burton, Dave King
Animals supplied by Trevor Smith's Animal World; Clubb-Chipperfield
Limited (pp 10-11, 22-23); Dorking Aquatics (pp 28-29).
Editorial consultant Joyce Pope
Special thanks to Carl Gombrich for research

This is a Borzoi Book published by Alfred A. Knopf, Inc.

The publishers would like to thank Premaphotos Wildlife/Ken Preston-Mafham
for their kind permission to reproduce the photograph on pp. 8-9.

Library of Congress Cataloging in Publication Data
Sowler, Sandie.
Amazing animal disguises / written by Sandie Sowler.
p. cm. – (Eyewitness juniors; 19)
Includes index.
Summary: Introduces animal disguises involving camouflage and
mimicry, in such animals as the zebra, polar bear, and caterpillar.

1. Camouflage (Biology) – Juvenile literature. 2. Mimicry (Biology) – Juvenile
literature [1. Camouflage (Biology) 2. Mimicry (Biology)]
I. Title. II. Series.
QL767.S68 1992 591.57'2–dc20 91-53141
ISBN 0-679-82768-4
ISBN 0-679-92768-9

Color reproduction by Colourscan, Singapore
Printed in Italy by A. Mondadori Editore, Verona

Contents

Why use a disguise? 8

Breaking up the shape 10

Snow white 12

Colorful creatures 14

Imitation 16

Mimicry 18

Disguised eyes 20

Hidden hunters 22

Camouflage for the young 24

Play-acting 26

Under cover 28

Index 29

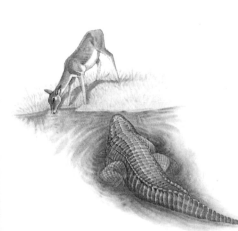

Why use a disguise?

From the moment a creature is born it must eat, and try to avoid being eaten. Most animals use some form of disguise, or camouflage, which helps to hide them among their surroundings.

Stony appearance
Oystercatchers nest on beaches. Their eggs are speckled and look like the stones around them. This disguise protects the delicate eggs during the four weeks before the chicks hatch.

Spotted or not?
Spots, stripes, and blotches merge an animal into its surroundings. The genet has a spotted fur coat. It is nocturnal, which means it is active at night. Since it sleeps during the day, it is easy prey, so its camouflage is extra important.

Flower-like growths on body

This mantis is 1 1/2 inches long

Flower power

Disguise is as useful for the hunter as it is for the hunted. This young, insect-eating mantis from Kenya is disguised as a colorful flower. But an insect visiting this "flower" would get a nasty shock!

Blending in

An animal that is the same color as its background is hard to see. All Arctic foxes are brown in summer, but some live in places which are covered by snow in winter. In winter these foxes grow white coats, so they are camouflaged all year round.

Head this way

This butterfly from Malaysia seems to have two heads. The headlike pattern on its rear wings can make a bird wonder which end to strike at!

Hopping twig

Some insects with no form of self-defense imitate something insect eaters do not eat. This treehopper has amazing twiglike growths on its back, making it look like a piece of tasteless wood.

Forelegs used for snatching prey

Sting in the tail

Predators tend to avoid poisonous animals. This harmless young stick insect strikes a scorpion-like pose when threatened, as if it had a poisonous sting in its tail.

Breaking up the shape

Bold stripes and spots are not only pretty to us but also useful to the animals that have them. The markings disguise the animal's shape by breaking it up into blocks of color. Watchful hunters can be very confused by what they are looking at!

Just like Mom
Young zebras are striped from birth. They can hide with Mom in the herd, where the stripes of all the zebras blend together.

Wrapped up
Ring-tailed lemurs rest in the trees during the day, wrapping their thick, black-and-white banded tail around them. The tail acts like a cloak to hide the lemur in the patches of light and shade in the tree.

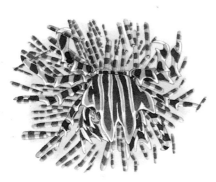

Anyone for leapfrog?
This striped frog lives in long grass. If its stripes don't hide it, it can jump out of danger with leaps of up to 15 feet.

A prickly bed
The striped pattern of the Adams' urchin crab camouflages it on the sea urchins on which it lives. The crab clings to the urchin's spines with a special hook on the end of its spiny legs.

Dotty runner
Guinea fowls live in flocks. They prefer to run rather than fly, but if they are attacked they fly up into the trees, where their spotted feathers make them difficult to see.

Seen in patches

The giraffe's long shape is disguised by a patchwork coat of dark and light brown. This helps it to hide among the trees of its African home.

Shapeless outfit

Zebras live on the African grasslands, where lions are often out looking for a meal. But a lion can be confused by a zebra's stripes, which in bright daylight can disguise the zebra's shape. In the dim light of dawn or dusk, the stripes seem to merge together and help the zebras to blend into the background.

This Chapman's zebra is 4½ ft tall at the shoulder

Snow white

In the snow, animals with dark coats would be seen easily. Many creatures grow a white coat to help them hide from enemies. Some are white or pale-colored all year round. Others change the color of their coat to suit the season.

Ladies first

In spring, ptarmigans start to grow their speckled brown summer coat. But the male will keep his white winter coat longer than the female. This means hunters see him before the well-camouflaged female, sitting on her eggs.

Winter woollies

The snow leopard lives high up in the Himalaya Mountains in Asia, where its beautiful coat hides it well in the snow. But the snow leopard is now very rare because some people kill leopards to sell their fur.

Big feet

The snowshoe hare has snow-white fur and has to move through deep snow to find food. To help it do this, it has wide, padded feet that are just like snowshoes!

Out for dinner

In winter, the varying lemming lives underground, where it is warmer. It comes out only to find food. Its white winter coat hides it from other animals who are hunting – for lemmings!

Turncoat

In winter, the stoat's coat changes from brown to white, but the tip of its tail stays black. Its name changes too – to ermine.

Nose guard

Some people say they have seen a polar bear cover its black nose with a paw when hunting, making itself white all over. But this has never been proved.

This snowy owl is 18 inches long from beak to tail

Snowy owl

The handsome snowy owl lives in the Arctic. Its thick, white, downy feathers keep it warm and camouflage it as it hunts for lemmings, hares, and fish.

Colorful creatures

Some animals have color cells in their skin that allow them to change their skin color. They do this to blend with their background, to show emotion, and to cool down or heat up.

Wet day   *Dry day*

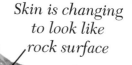

Skin is changing to look like rock surface

Two-color toad
The common toad lives on the forest floor. On a dry day, its skin is light brown to match the dry leaves and soil. But when rain falls and darkens the ground, the toad's skin darkens too.

Jet set
The octopus can change the color, and even the texture, of its skin. When it moves onto a rock to rest, not only does its skin color match the rock's coloring, but its skin gets bumpy too, just like the rock's surface.

Check mate
A dab is a flatfish that lives on the seabed. As it moves across the seabed, its skin color can change to match the background. If it were placed on a chess board, the fish would even become checkered!

Quick change
The cuttlefish changes color quickly, which is useful when it is hunting. Waves of color and changing patterns pass over its body. This distracts or confuses its prey.

Matching dress
The crab spider can change its color to match the flower it is sitting on. Its perfect camouflage hides it from insects when they settle on the flower to feed. Then the spider catches *them* for dinner.

Colorful character

Of all the color-change creatures, chameleons have the widest color range. To blend in with their surroundings, their skin color can include black, brown, yellow, green, blue, and even bright red. They also change color when cold, hot, threatened – or in love!

Horns are used when fighting rival males

This male Jackson's chameleon is 1 foot long

The Jackson's chameleon lives in the mountain forests of eastern Africa

Imitation

Many animals don't look like animals at all. Instead, they mimic, or imitate, something their enemies would overlook or never eat.

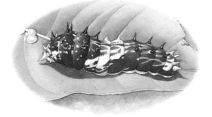

Fishy story

The leafy sea dragon is a strange kind of sea horse. It avoids being noticed by camouflaging itself as a piece of seaweed. To complete the disguise, it often clings to real seaweed.

Clever caterpillar

Who would want to eat a bird dropping? That's what the caterpillar of the king page butterfly is disguised as. If it keeps still, it's not likely to appear on any animal's menu!

Stumped!

The potoo hunts by night and rests during the day. To sleep safely, this bird finds a tree stump and sits bolt upright on the end of it, as if it were part of the stump. An enemy has to look extra hard to find it!

Insect's skin looks like the skin of a real leaf

Leg

Imitation midrib

Imitation vein

Leaf with legs

The Javanese leaf insect is an amazing imitation of a real leaf. It has markings which look like the midrib and veins of a real leaf, and brown markings like a leaf that is dying.

Marks on
body look like
holes in a
dying leaf

Head

Real
leaf

Thorny problem

It's a problem spotting thorn bugs, particularly when there are several on one branch. They look exactly like rose thorns and often fool a hungry bird.

These Javanese leaf insects are 3 inches long

When resting, Javanese leaf insects settle on a tree branch and curl their bodies to look like the other leaves on the branch

Stick insect

Certain insects, such as this South American grasshopper, mimic sticks. Many add to their disguise by swaying gently, as if caught in a light breeze.

Leafy leaper

The Asian horned frog lives on the forest floor. Its brown, leafy camouflage hides it among the leaf litter as it waits for any prey that might pass by.

Mimicry

Hunters learn to avoid animals that are unpleasant or poisonous. Many harmless animals mimic, or look like, harmful animals as a form of protection.

Rosy cheeks

The mountain dusky salamander is usually a dull brown color all over. But in areas where the horrible-tasting red-cheeked salamander lives, the dusky salamander has red cheeks too.

Ant mimic

Ants can bite, sting, and squirt acid, so most insect eaters leave them alone. Many insects mimic ants. This amazing insect is a treehopper. Part of its body is shaped exactly like an ant, and the rest of it blends in with the leaf it is sitting on.

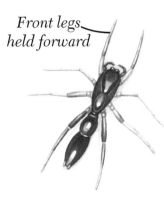

Front legs held forward

Jumping ant

This jumping spider is an ant mimic. It has a slim, antlike body, and because spiders have eight legs and ants only six legs, this spider holds its two front legs forward and waves them so they look like ant feelers.

Not so loving

When a firefly wants to mate, it flashes light signals. Every species of firefly has its own special signal. The female of one type of firefly attracts males of a different species by mimicking their signal. When a male settles next to the female to mate – she eats him!

False alarm

Any animal that has been stung by a real wasp is unlikely to mess with one again. The clearwing moth is a wasp mimic. It adds to its disguise by making a wasplike buzzing noise.

Waspish look-alike

This hover fly, with its striped black and yellow jacket, looks like a wasp but has no sting. It lives and feeds among flowers and rotting fruit, just like real wasps.

This hover fly is ¹/₂ inch long

Wasplike yellow and black stripes

Cockroach

Ladybug

Ladylike

A ladybug may look pretty to us, but its bright red and black coloring warns hunters that it tastes awful. This cockroach would make a nice snack for an insect eater, but since it looks just like a ladybug, hunters will probably leave it alone.

Making an ass of himself

In an Aesop's fable, an ass put on a lion's skin he had found in the forest. He had great fun scaring all the other forest creatures, who thought he was a real lion. But one day, a fox laughed at him. He had heard the ass's voice and discovered who he was.

19

Disguised eyes

Eyes can give their owner away to the enemy when they catch the light. Special stripes and patterns on the head help many animals to hide their eyes. Some animals even have "false eyes" somewhere else on their body to add to the disguise.

Eyes on the back of its head
No matter which way its head is turned, the pearl-spotted owlet seems to be watching you. The two spots on the back of its head could easily be mistaken for real eyes.

Eye escaped
The eyespots on this butterfly's wings must have looked like real eyes to somebody. The butterfly was attacked, but the enemy went for the wrong eyes and the butterfly survived.

Flasher

When this silkmoth opens its front wings to fly off, a hungry bird would be startled by the sudden appearance of two eyespots on the moth's hind wings.

Assault and battery?

Wahlberg's epauletted fruit bats rest together in trees. To protect their special night-seeing eyes from the claws of bad-tempered neighbors, they have white tufts under their ears that act as decoy eyes.

Shocking end

The caterpillar of this Costa Rican moth has a rear end that looks just like the head of a tiny viper, with two large, scary, black eyes. Any creature that goes too close gets a nasty shock!

Heads I win, tails you lose!

The copperband butterfly fish not only makes an enemy think its tail is its head, but also hides its real eyes in a dark, vertical stripe, so the enemy is likely to snap at the wrong end.

This copperband butterfly fish is 3 inches long

Two-faced cobra

A cobra spreads its "hood" when it wants to look frightening. The two eyespots on the back of the hood may startle an enemy long enough for the cobra to escape.

Hidden hunters

Hunters use camouflage so they can pounce on their prey before the prey sees them. Some sneak up on their meal. Others keep very still and wait for a meal to come to them!

This tiger is 8 feet 9 inches long from the tip of its nose to the tip of its tail

Telltale tail
Leopards often rest in trees during the day, their spotted coat blending with the branches and leaves. But one thing that may give them away is their long tail.

Praying or preying?
Looking like the leaves on which it sits, this praying mantis can stay still for hours, almost as if it were praying. Then, in a flash, it strikes at any prey that comes too close.

Deadly twig
The vine snake lives in the jungle and twists its long, thin body around the branches of trees. It looks like a harmless piece of jungle vine as it waits for its supper to arrive.

Cover-up

In India, leopards are thought to be very cunning. Legend has it that they brush away their own tracks with their tail!

Creepy crocodile

The crocodile's murky brown coloring disguises it in the water where it hunts. It swims slowly up to its prey, then drags it into the water and holds it under until it drowns.

Patient killer

When a heron hunts, it stands as still as a statue, waiting patiently for a fish to pass close by. When the fish is in range, the heron suddenly snatches it with its long beak.

Deerstalker

The tiger stalks its prey slowly and carefully, its striped coat camouflaging it in the long grass. Then, with a sudden bound, it goes for the kill.

When the tiger stalks prey, it draws in its sharp claws so it can creep up silently on its padded feet

Camouflage for the young

Young animals are usually weak and defenseless, so camouflage is of extra importance to them. Some are born with the same camouflage as their parents, while others have their own special disguise until they become adults.

Hide and seek

Unlike their parents, lion cubs have spotted coats. When the mother lion hunts for food, she has to leave the cubs behind. The spots help the cubs to blend with the shady patches under the trees where they hide.

Icy nursery

Until a seal pup, like this harp seal pup with an adult male, is old enough to swim, it stays on land. A seal pup has a white coat to camouflage it in its snowy Arctic home. When the pup is old enough to start swimming, it loses its white coat.

Keep your head down!

Most young deer, like this white-tailed deer, have spotted coats that hide them in the light and shade of the forest. As this white-tailed deer becomes older and able to run from danger instead of hiding, it will lose its spots.

These pheasant chicks are about 2 inches tall

Pleasant pheasants

These fluffy pheasant chicks have light- and dark-brown feathers to match the ground where their nest is. These chicks are only two days old. They will be able to fly after about 12 days.

Changing room

At the stage when a caterpillar is changing into a butterfly, it is known as a pupa. It stays in one place at this time, so the pupa must be well camouflaged. This pupa of the citrus swallowtail butterfly looks just like a leaf.

All white in the end

There is a story about an ugly duckling who was teased because he was so ugly, and not yellow and fluffy like the other ducklings. But when he grew up, he wasn't a duck at all. He lost his dull gray coat and became a beautiful swan.

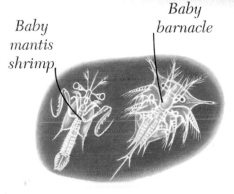

Baby mantis shrimp

Baby barnacle

See-through babies

The young of barnacles, crabs, and many other sea creatures are tiny and transparent and have the most amazing shapes. They float near the surface of the sea, where it is very bright, so their see-through bodies give them the best protection.

Play-acting

To protect themselves and their young, or to get a better chance of grabbing a meal, animals can be the most amazing actors.

A clean bite

Cleaner fish remove insects that live on other fishes' bodies. The saber-toothed blenny mimics the cleaner fish and advertises itself by doing the cleaner fish's special zigzag dance. But when a fish goes up to be cleaned, the blenny takes a bite of flesh instead!

Putting on an act

If a ringed plover sitting on its nest of eggs or chicks spots a hunter, it acts quickly. It pretends to have a broken wing and leads the hunter, who thinks the injured plover is an easy meal, far away from the nest. The plover then suddenly flies off to safety.

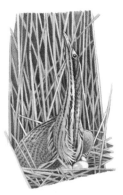

Stretch and sway

When the bittern senses danger, it stretches its neck and points its head to the sky. This makes it almost impossible to see among the reedy marshland. And if the reeds are swaying in a breeze, the bird will sway too.

This hognose snake is 3 feet long

Sneaky snake

The young cottonmouth snake is completely camouflaged except for a bright yellow tip at the end of its tail. It wiggles this tip to attract frogs, who think it is something small and tasty for them to eat. What a mistake!

Faint-hearted

Every time the fainting goat is threatened, it faints! The faint lasts for less than a minute, then the goat gets up. People in the United States keep the goat as a pet but it could not survive in the wild. And the advantage it gets from fainting has never been discovered.

Dead or alive?

If the hognose snake is threatened, it pretends to die. It turns upside-down and throws back its head, holding its mouth open. Lots of animals do this to save themselves, as many hunters like to kill their food themselves. This way they know they have fresh meat.

1. Run for your life...

The opossum is famous for faking death. Here an American opossum is being chased by a dog, but it can't run fast enough, and the dog soon catches up.

2. Sudden death...

With no escape, the opossum drops to the ground, rolls over, and looks as if it has died. Its mouth is hanging open, and its eyes are glassy and staring.

3. What a recovery!

The dog now thinks the opossum is dead and will not eat it. Soon the dog goes away. Once all is clear, the opossum gets up and scurries off.

Under cover

One way of hiding from enemies – or from prey – is to wear a fancy dress. Some animals use sticks, stones, plants, and even other animals to disguise themselves and protect their body from attack.

Say cheese!
The only thing that could give away the presence of a stargazer fish as it lies buried beneath the sand is its toothy grin. Should a fish pass by too close, it is quickly snapped up.

Gardener wanted!
In the misty forests of New Guinea, several types of weevils grow gardens of small plants on their backs for camouflage. And like all gardens, their gardens have insects!

A stitch in time
Crickets are active by night and rest by day. Each day, this wingless cricket makes a new house to hide in. It does this by cutting a piece of leaf, rolling it around itself like a blanket, and then "stitching" the edges together with silk thread made by glands in its lip.

Silk thread

Shell suit
Sea urchins are well protected by their spines, but they can still be eaten. Some urchins take bits of shells, pebbles, and seaweed and arrange them over their bodies. This disguise hides urchins from enemies and also protects them from the sun in shallow waters.

Mobile graveyard

Some lacewing grubs have a grisly way of hiding. They suck the juices out of their greenfly victims and then stick the remains on their backs.

Greenfly corpses

Not just for decoration

The decorator crab covers its body with objects from the seabed. The seaweed, pieces of sponge, and mosses it uses for camouflage are held on by thousands of tiny hooked bristles which cover its entire body.

The decorator crab measures about 2 inches across its back

Index

ants   18
Arctic fox   9

bats   21
birds   8, 9, 10, 12, 16, 20, 23, 26
butterflies   9, 16, 20, 25

caterpillars   16, 25
crabs   10, 25, 28-29
crickets   28
crocodiles   23

deer   24

fainting goat   27
fireflies   18
fish   14, 20-21, 26, 28
frogs   10

genets   8
giraffes   11

hover flies   19

Jackson's chameleon   15
Javanese leaf insect   16-17

leafy sea dragon   16
lemmings   12
lemurs   10
leopards   12, 22, 23

mantises   8-9, 22
moths   21

octopuses   14
opossums   27

pheasants   24-25
polar bear   13

salamanders   18
seals   24
sea urchins   28
snakes   21, 22, 26-27
snowshoe hare   12
snowy owl   12-13
spiders   14, 18

thorn bugs   17
tiger   22-23
toads   14
treehoppers   9, 18

weevils   28

zebra   10-11

I Can DRAW
Sea Creatures

Walter Foster

Interiors illustrated by George Gaadt with Roy Schlemme

Here's what you need...

You're about to become an artist! Before you start, make sure you have a pencil, a pencil sharpener, an eraser, a felt-tip pen, and one or more of the different coloring media pictured here. Then, look in the back of the book for your grid pages. They'll help you to follow the special drawing steps. If you need more paper, you can ask a grown-up to help you to copy the grids.

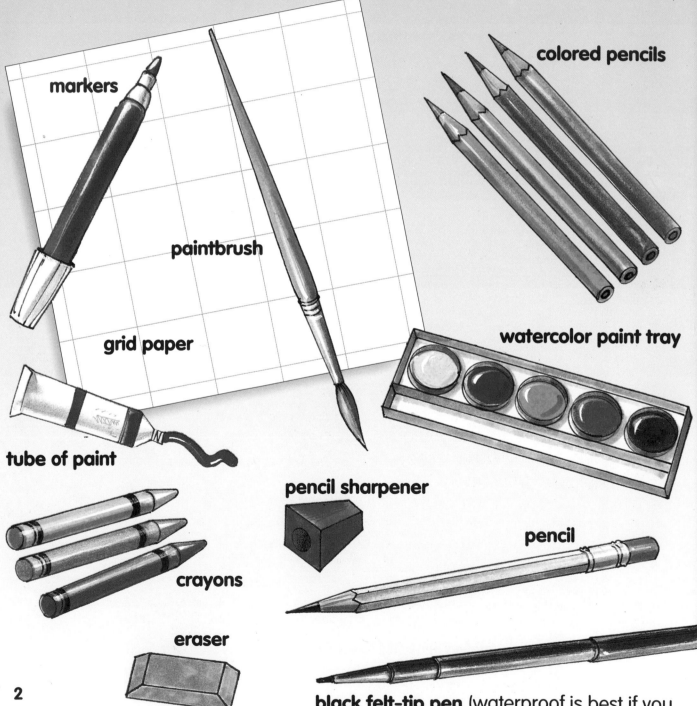

markers

paintbrush

grid paper

tube of paint

crayons

colored pencils

watercolor paint tray

pencil sharpener

pencil

eraser

2

black felt-tip pen (waterproof is best if you use watercolors to paint your drawings)

and here's what you do!

1 Copy each step-by-step drawing onto your grid paper, noticing where the drawing should touch the lines on your grid. Draw lightly in pencil. Since each new step is shown in blue, you'll always know exactly what to do next.

TIP: Be sure to start in the middle of the grid paper.

2 You may erase the pencil construction lines as you go along so that you can see how your drawing is progressing. When you have finished, use your felt-tip pen to go over the lines you want to keep, and erase any stray pencil lines.

Now you have a perfect drawing to color any way you'd like! Before you color, you may want to read pages 30 to 32 for some extra coloring tips.

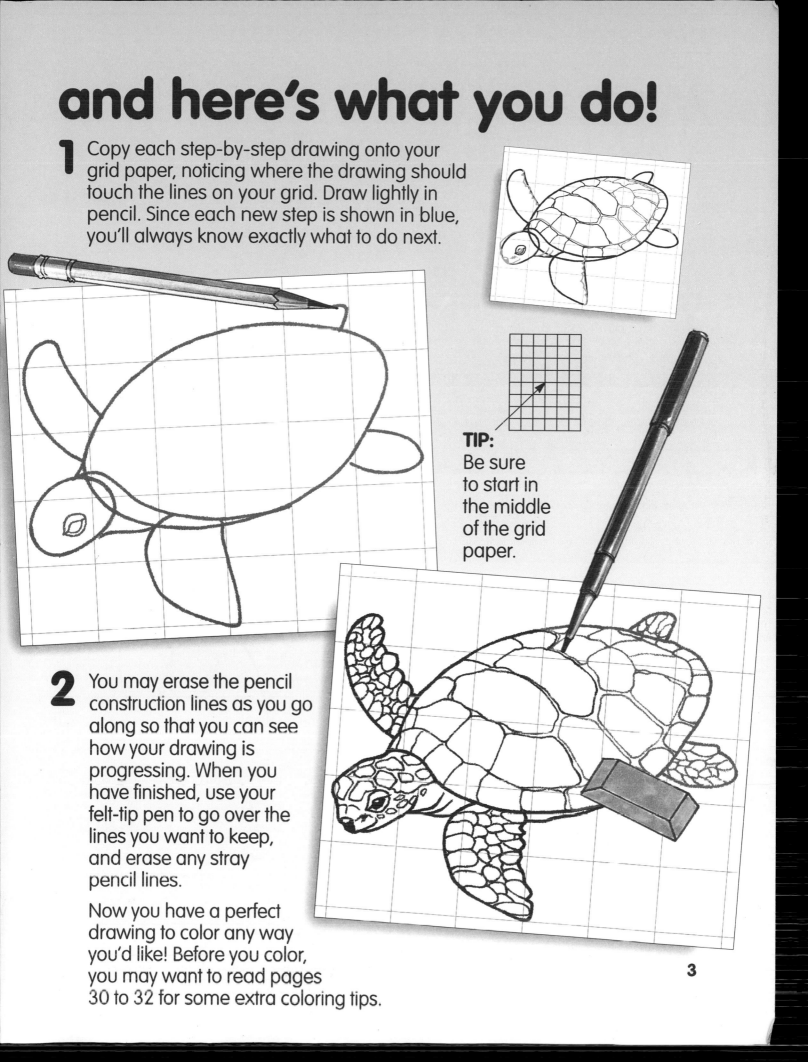

3

Manatee

1

Be sure to start in the middle of the grid paper. Draw the head and the body.

Add facial features, neck, belly, flippers, and tail.

2

3

Use your felt-tip pen to trace over the lines you want to keep, and erase the extra pencil lines.

4 Color your manatee!

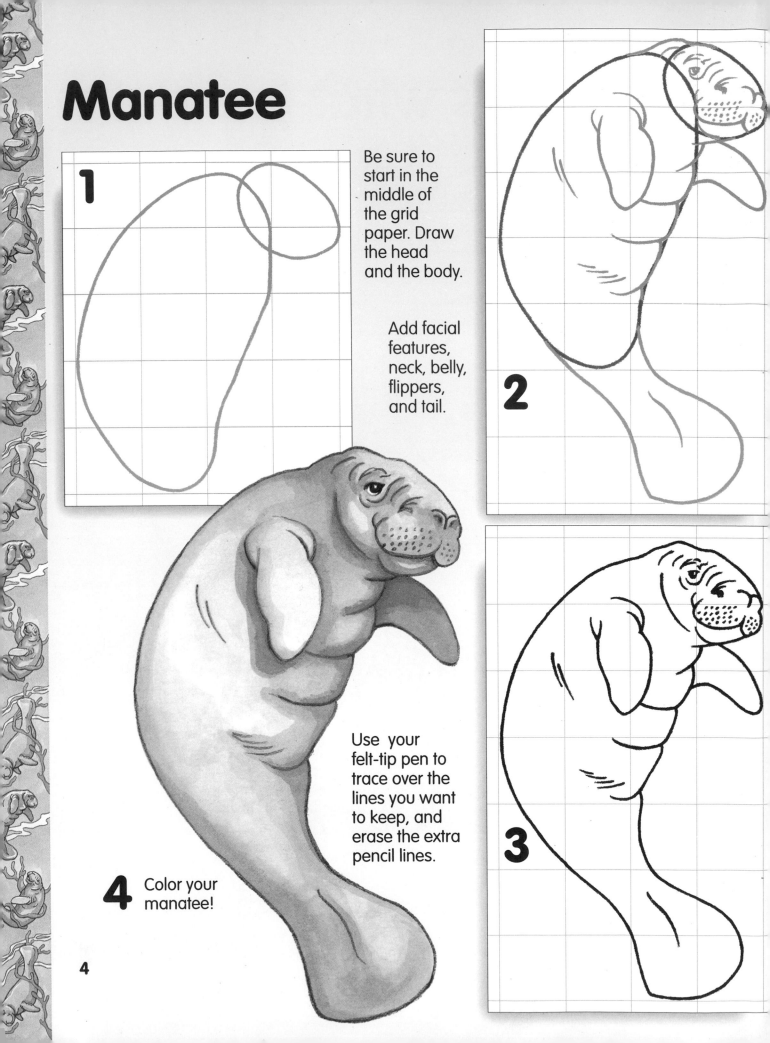

Eel

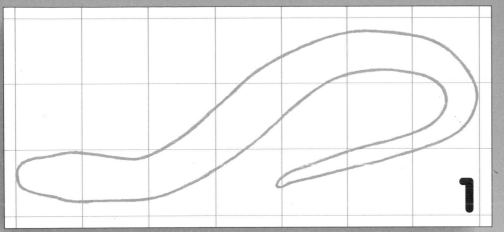

1 Draw your eel's body with long, curved lines.

Draw an eye, sharp teeth, and long fins on the top and bottom of your eel.

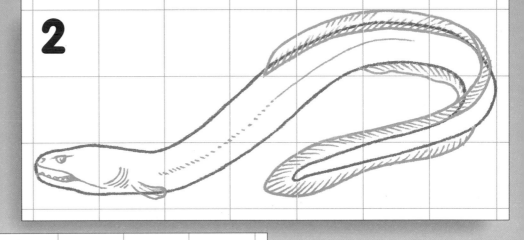

2

Use your felt-tip pen to trace over the lines you want to keep, and erase the extra pencil lines.

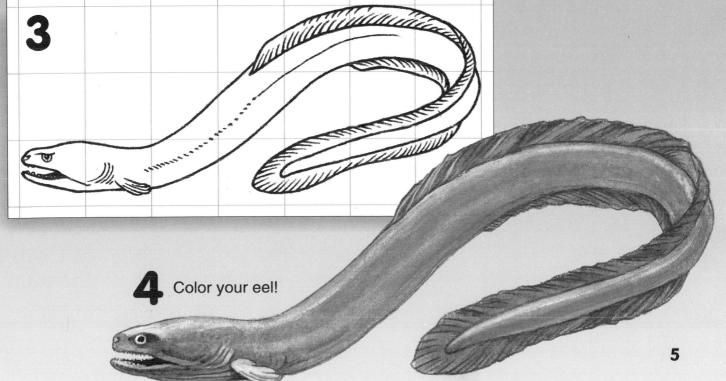

3

4 Color your eel!

5

Octopus

Add the suction cups to the tentacles. Fill in the details of the eye.

3

2

Give your octopus eight curly tentacles.

Be sure to start in the middle of the grid paper. Draw the body, the head, and an eye.

1

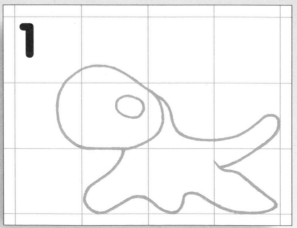

6

4 Draw spots on your octopus.

Here, your octopus is at rest. Later, you'll learn how to draw him in action.

5 Use your felt-tip pen to trace over the lines you want to keep, and erase the extra pencil lines.

6 Color your octopus!

Great White Shark

Use curved lines to draw the body. Add an eye.

1

Give your shark a sharp nose and a mouth. Draw a tail fin and two top fins.

2

Add details to the eye and mouth. Draw side and bottom fins.

3

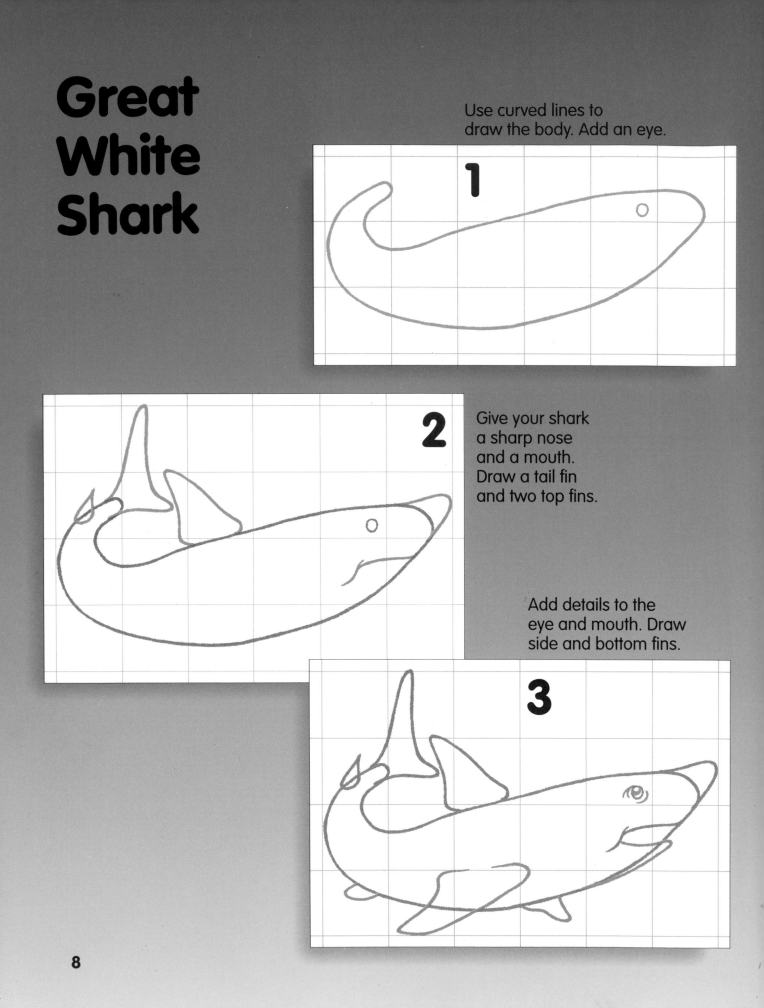

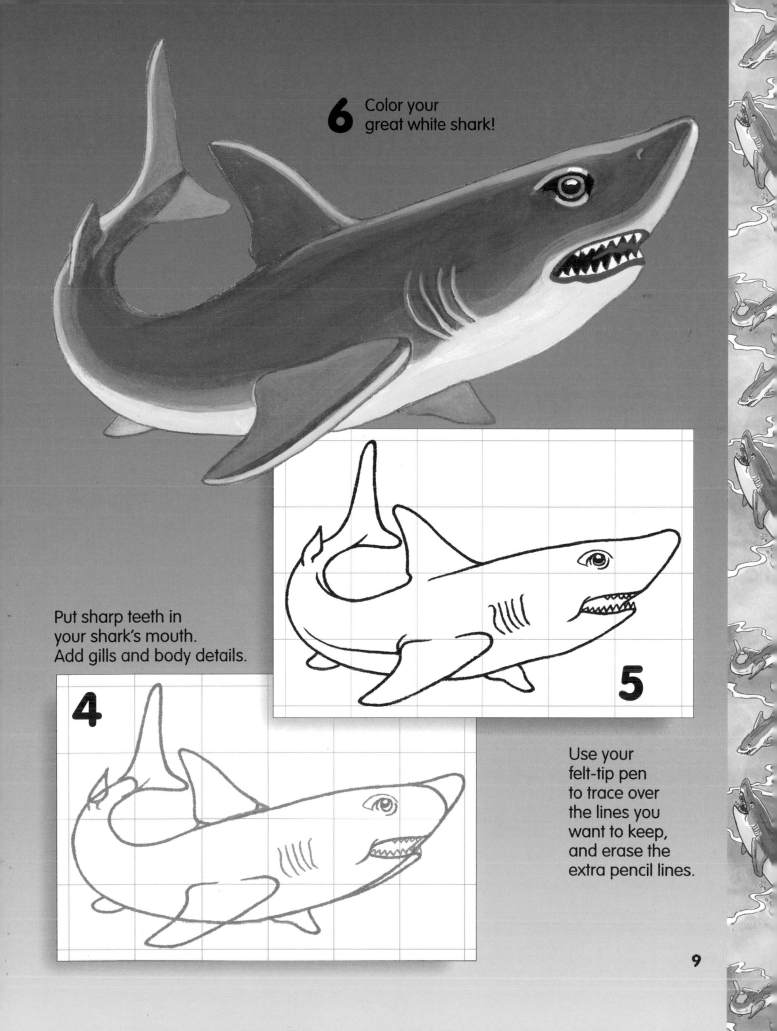

6 Color your
great white shark!

Put sharp teeth in
your shark's mouth.
Add gills and body details.

5

4

Use your
felt-tip pen
to trace over
the lines you
want to keep,
and erase the
extra pencil lines.

9

Sea Creatures in Action

Diving, swimming, or crawling, sea creatures are constantly in motion! Here's how to draw two sea creatures that move in very different ways.

The octopus moves its tentacles together and apart when it swims. (Learn how to draw the octopus on page 6.)

A dolphin flexes its body when it dives into the water. (Learn how to draw a dolphin on page 20.)

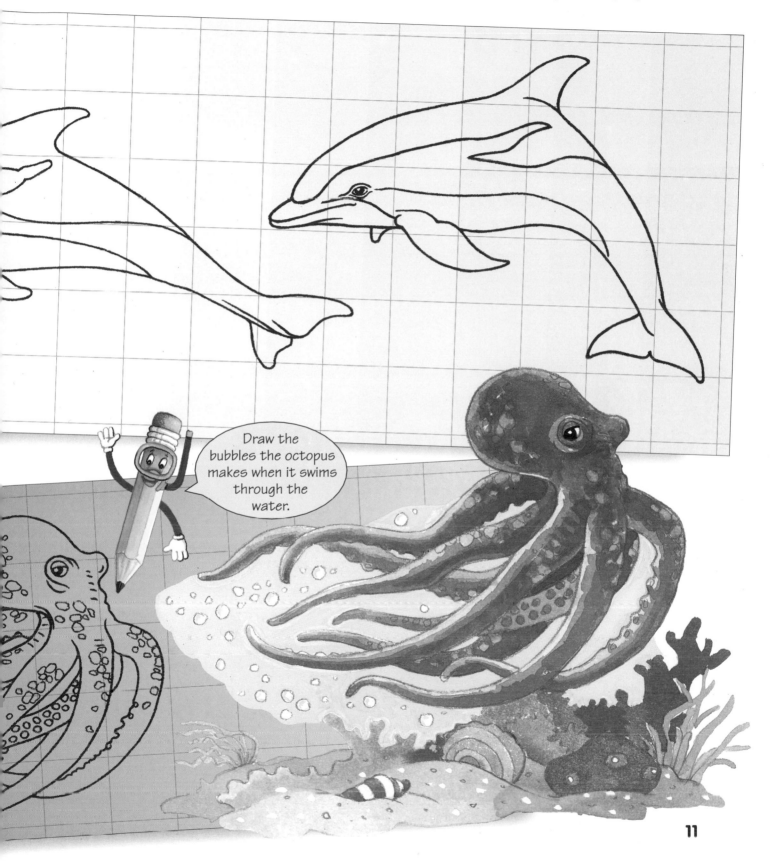

11

Crab

Give your crab eyes and a mouth. Add the bottom of the claws and four rear legs.

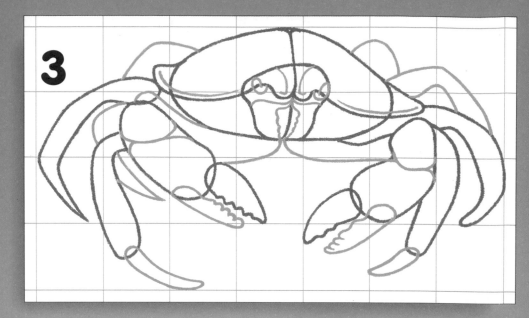

Add the top of the shell and four of the legs. Use jagged lines to make the edges of the claws.

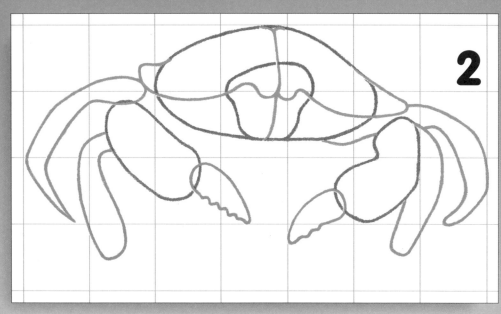

Be sure to start in the middle of the grid paper. Draw the body, a shape for the face, and the main parts of the front claws.

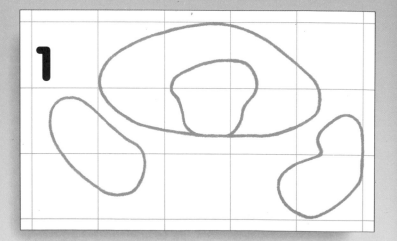

4 Add details on the face and legs.

Use your felt-tip pen to trace over the lines you want to keep, and erase the extra pencil lines.

5

6 Color your crab!

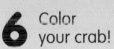

Sea Turtle

3

Use small, uneven lines to draw the back of the flippers. Add the shell, head and eye details, and a mouth.

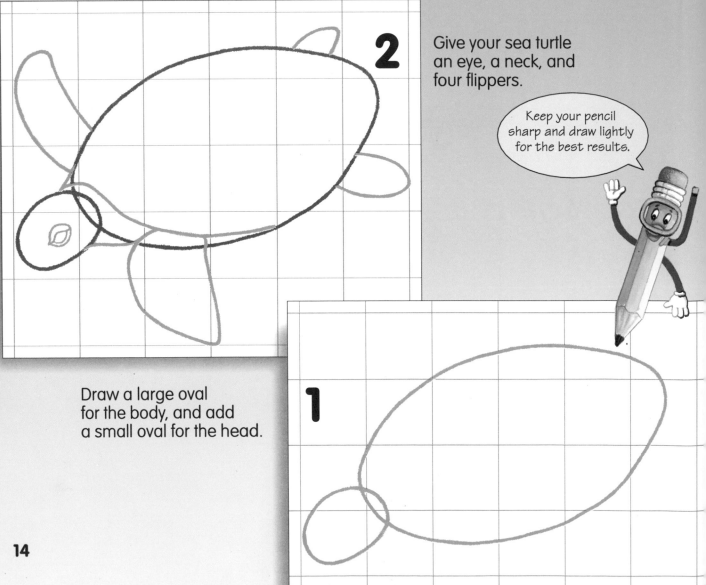

2

Give your sea turtle an eye, a neck, and four flippers.

Keep your pencil sharp and draw lightly for the best results.

Draw a large oval for the body, and add a small oval for the head.

1

Use your felt-tip pen to trace over the lines you want to keep, and erase the extra pencil lines.

5

4

Fill in the details on the sea turtle's shell, flippers, and head.

6 Color your sea turtle!

15

Making Backgrounds

You can add background scenes to make your sea creatures even more realistic and exciting and to help your pictures get noticed. Try copying the backgrounds shown here, and then make up some of your own!

Learn to draw a sea turtle on page 14. ▲

Learn to draw a shark on page 8. ▲

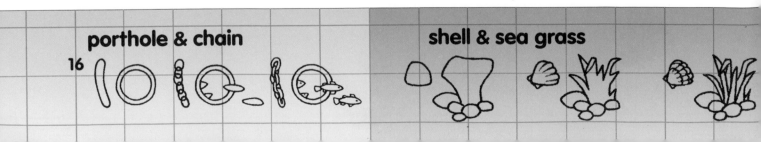

porthole & chain

shell & sea grass

Learn to draw a seal on page 22. ▲

Learn to draw tropical fish on page 18. ▲

Learn to draw a crab on page 12. ▲

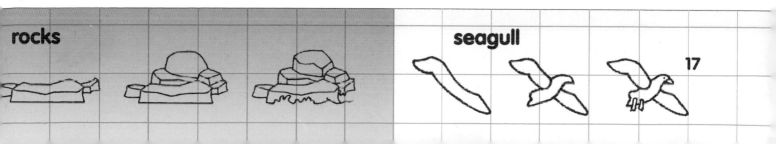

rocks

seagull

17

Tropical Fish

Add eyes, mouths, and side fins. Give the sea horse a neck and a tail.

2

1

Draw the bodies and tail fins of the clown anemone fish and moorish idol. Draw the head and body of the sea horse.

3

Draw more fins and darken the eyes. Add details to the tails, fins, and faces.

Clown Anemone Fish

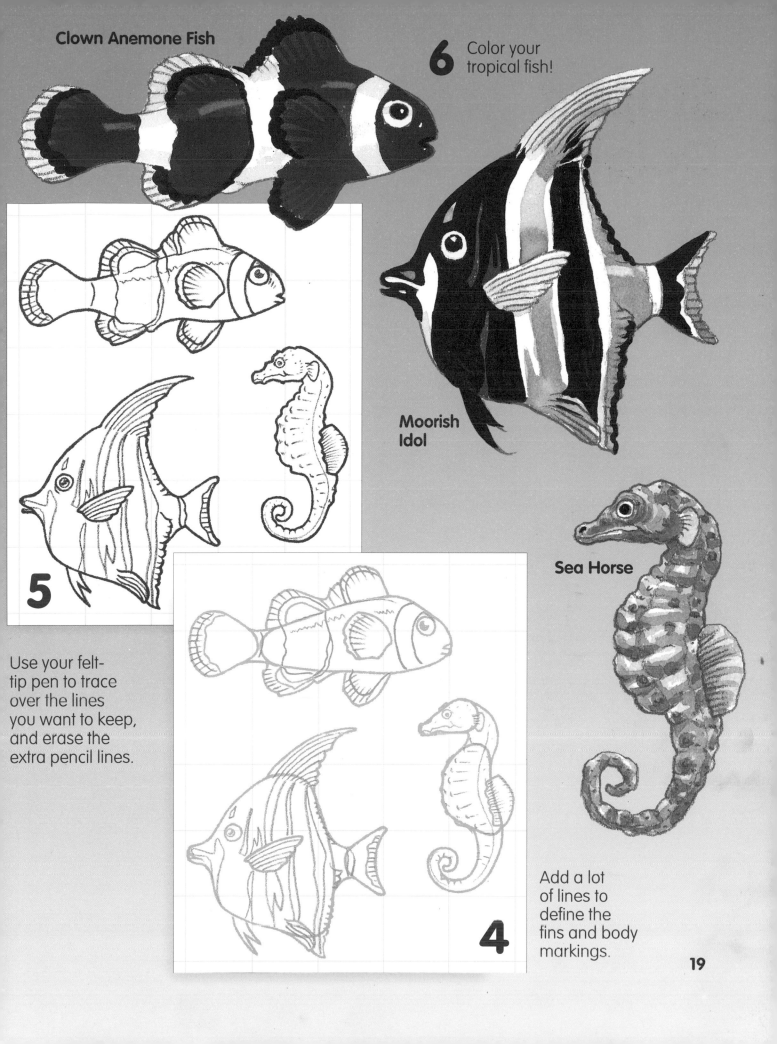

Moorish Idol

Sea Horse

5

Use your felt-tip pen to trace over the lines you want to keep, and erase the extra pencil lines.

Add a lot of lines to define the fins and body markings.

4

19

Striped Dolphin

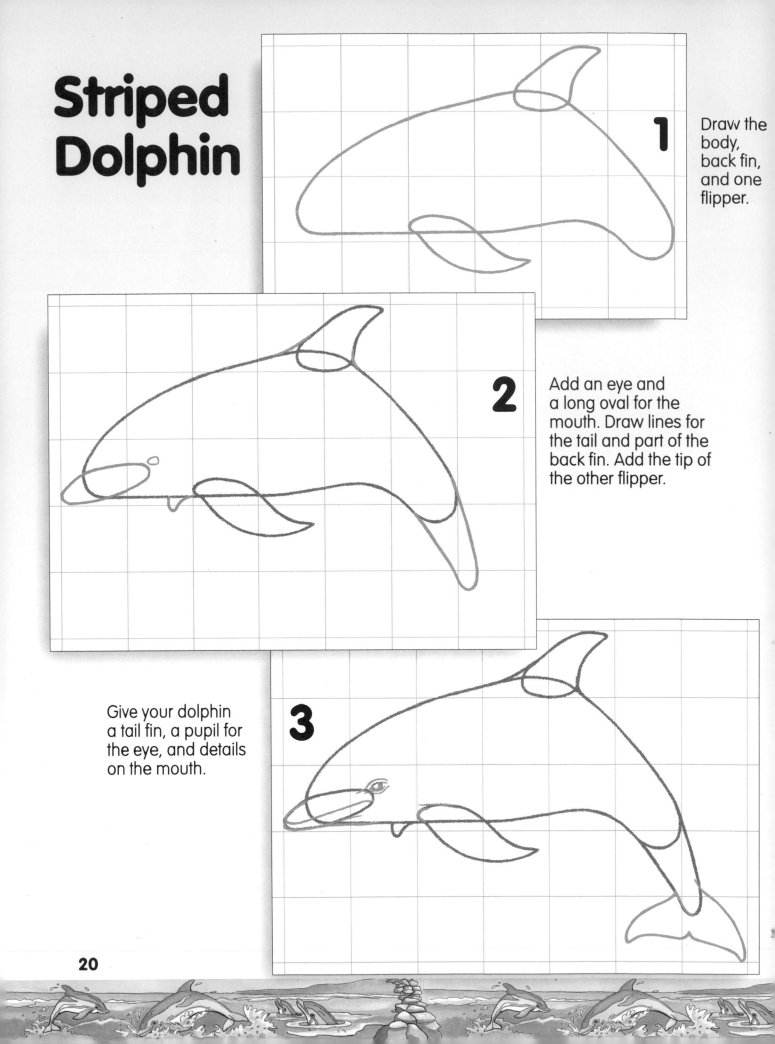

1 Draw the body, back fin, and one flipper.

2 Add an eye and a long oval for the mouth. Draw lines for the tail and part of the back fin. Add the tip of the other flipper.

Give your dolphin a tail fin, a pupil for the eye, and details on the mouth.

3

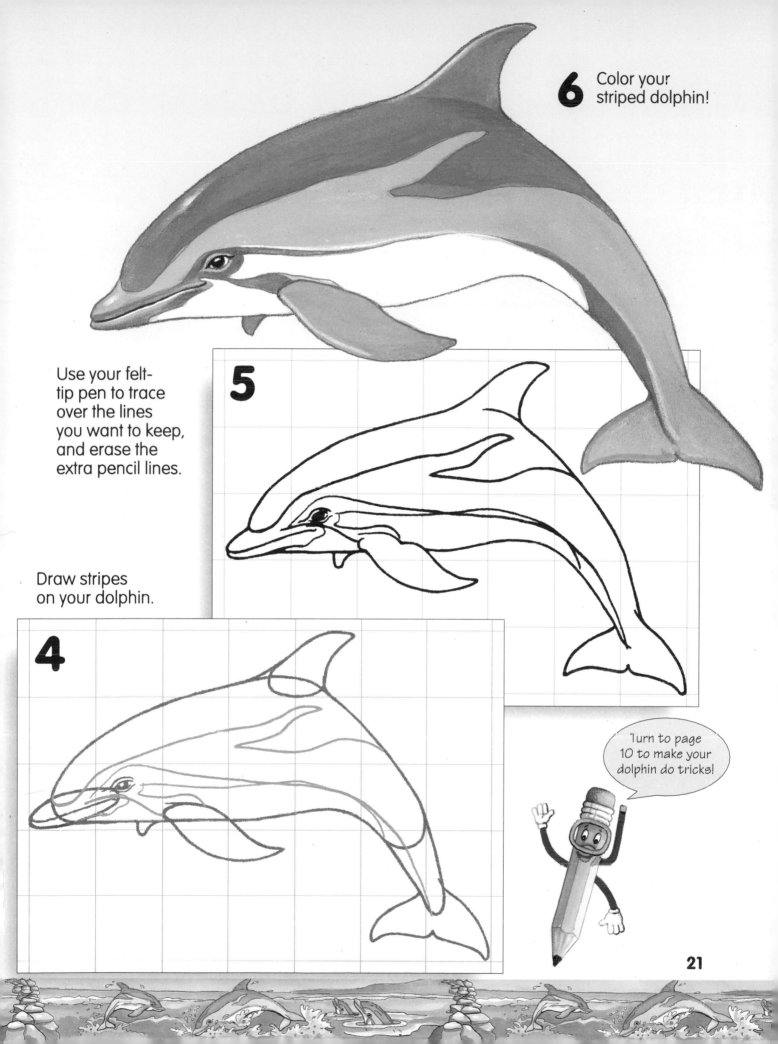

6 Color your striped dolphin!

Use your felt-tip pen to trace over the lines you want to keep, and erase the extra pencil lines.

5

Draw stripes on your dolphin.

4

Turn to page 10 to make your dolphin do tricks!

21

Seal

Give your seal front flippers, an eye, an ear, and a mouth.

3

2 Add the snout, neck, and tail.

Draw the body, and make a circle for the head.

1

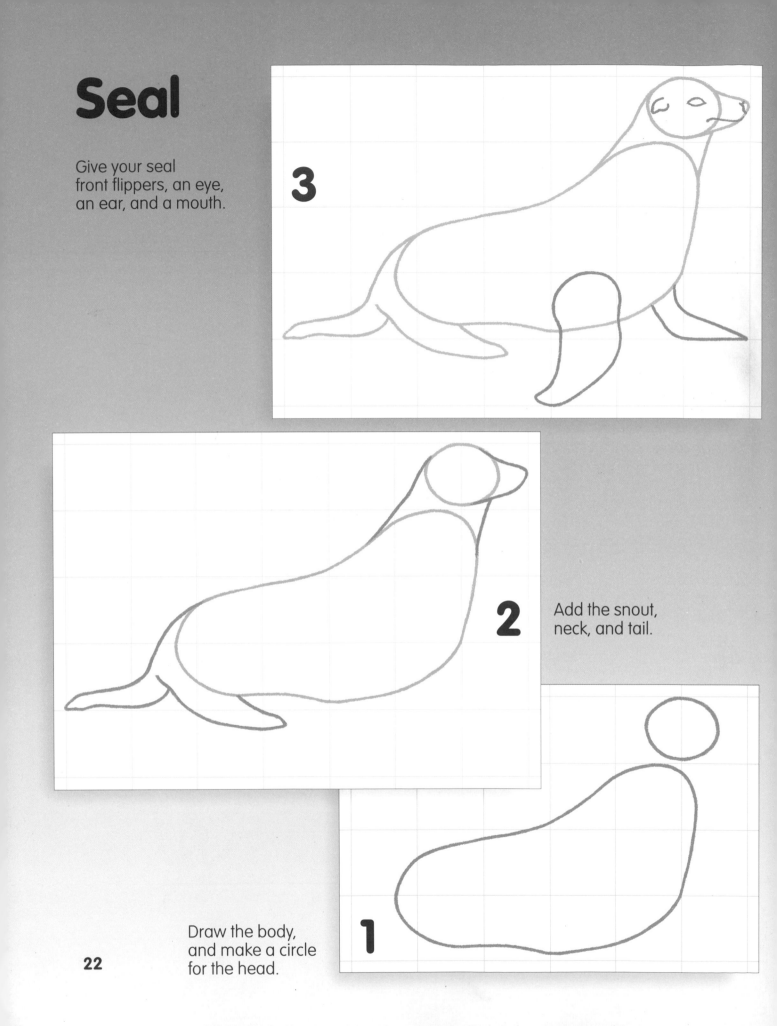

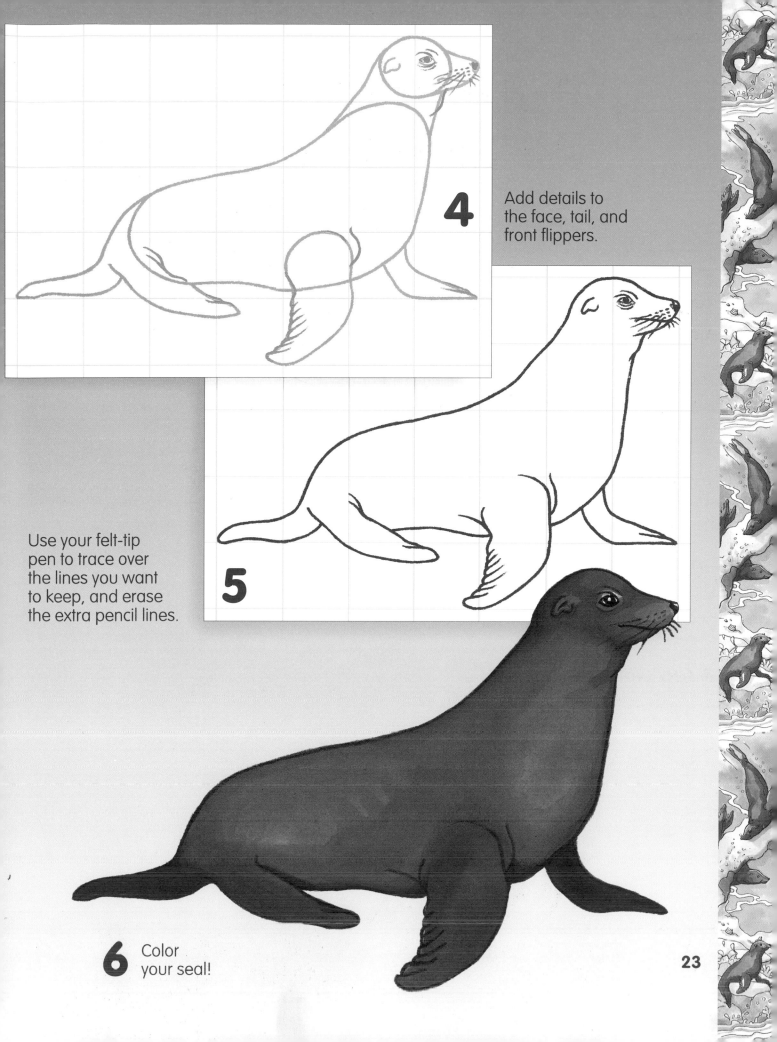

4 Add details to the face, tail, and front flippers.

5 Use your felt-tip pen to trace over the lines you want to keep, and erase the extra pencil lines.

6 Color your seal!

23

Putting It All Together

Now you're ready to create a scene by putting different sea creatures together and building a background around them. All the creatures in this book wouldn't really live in the same part of the sea, but you're the artist, so go ahead and put your scenes together any way you'd like!

Lobster

Add a circle for the head and a cone shape for the feelers. Then add legs, a tail, and eyes. Use small, curved lines to shape the body.

Draw the antennae. Darken the eyes. Add jaws, body lines, leg joints, and "teeth" on the claws.

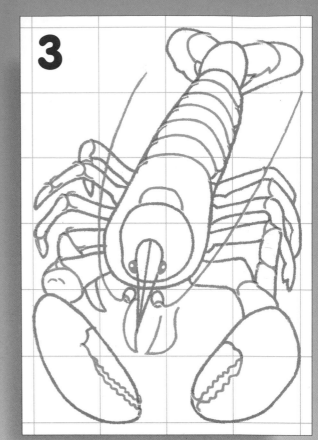

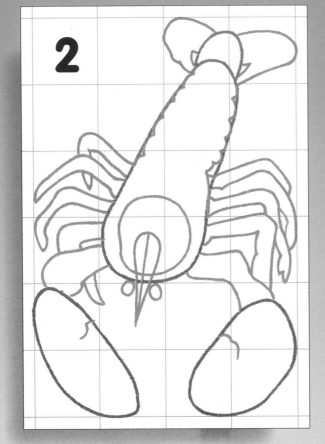

Draw the body and the two front claws.

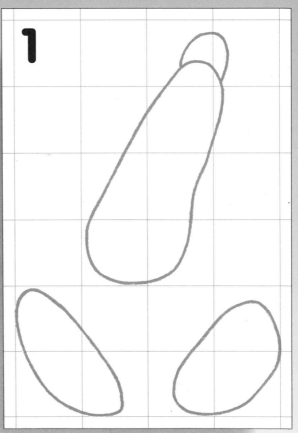

Use your felt-tip pen to trace over the lines you want to keep, and erase the extra pencil lines.

Put spots on your lobster's body and claws. Add details to the face, tail, and antennae.

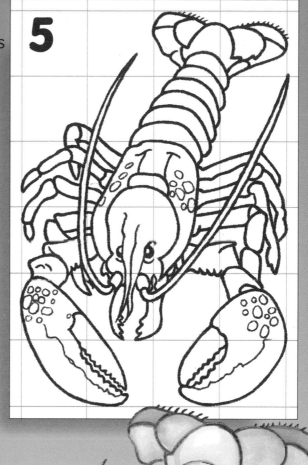

5

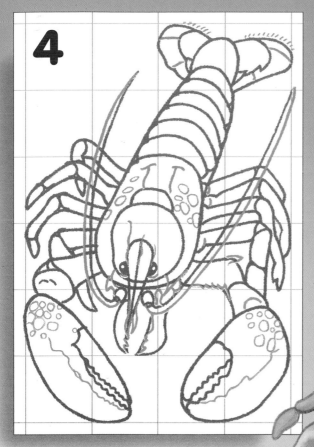

4

6 Color your lobster!

27

Killer Whale

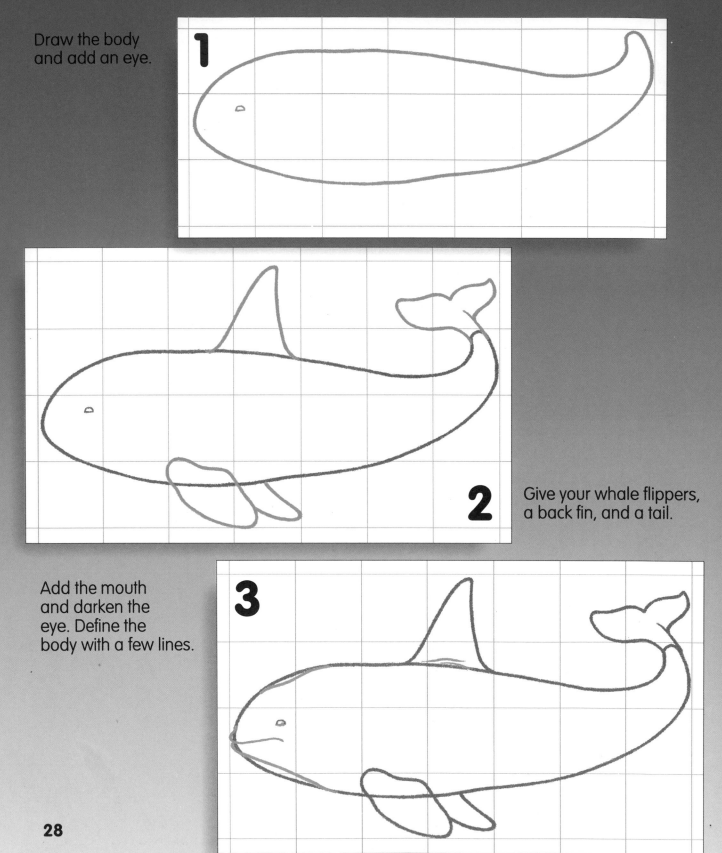

Draw the body and add an eye.

1

Give your whale flippers, a back fin, and a tail.

2

Add the mouth and darken the eye. Define the body with a few lines.

3

28

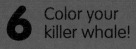

6 Color your
killer whale!

Use your felt-tip
pen to trace over
the lines you want
to keep, and erase
the extra pencil lines.

5

4 Add details
around the eye
and on the body.

Coloring Your Drawings

Once you've finished the outlines of your drawings, it's fun to color them in. Use watercolor paints, colored pencils, crayons, markers, or anything else you can think of!

Watercolors are fun to use, but sometimes when two wet paint colors are next to one another, they run together. If you're using watercolors, you will want to let the paint dry after each color you use.

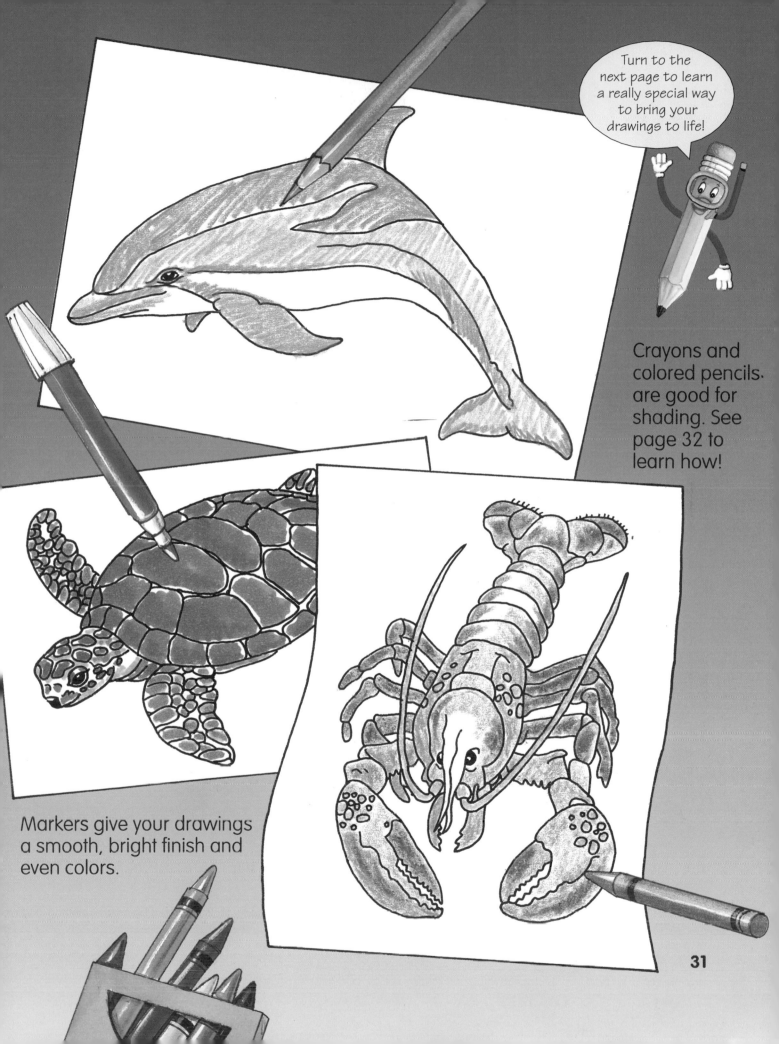

Turn to the next page to learn a really special way to bring your drawings to life!

Crayons and colored pencils are good for shading. See page 32 to learn how!

Markers give your drawings a smooth, bright finish and even colors.

31

Shading Your Drawings

Use these grid pages for your drawings. Make extra copies so you can draw a lot of pictures using the special steps in this book!

Shading can add dimension and life to your drawings. Try shading first with a crayon or colored pencil, using the side of the point. Make an area of your sea creature darker where there would be less light on it. The darker areas create shadows, which give your drawing a three-dimensional look.

32